POUNDING NAILS
IN THE FLOOR WITH MY FOREHEAD

ERIC BOGOSIAN

THEATRE COMMUNICATIONS GROUP

CONTENTS

For my parents, Edwina and Henry

I've written an introduction to this book which supposedly explains why I made the piece in the first place. It's probably a good idea not to read the introduction, because it leaves out alot. I don't really know why I make what I make. Bottom line is, it's fun, all pretension aside. If you have to read this book for college credit, then maybe you should read the introduction. But I think the best way to read this book is after you've seen one of the shows.

Once upon a time, before television invaded our hearts and minds, the world stood as a mystery—huge and apart from us. One could, like Ulysses or Melville or Kerouac or Earhart (or Dennis Hopper in *Easy Rider*), go out and "find" the world, explore it a bit and, if you survived, come back to tell your hard-won tale. An explorer was a hero because the world was full of danger and its vastness awesome.

In the old days, people who weren't explorers learned about the world in bits and pieces. The world was "out there" and everyone carried within him or her a version of the world—a collage of old *National Geographic* pictorials, newspaper clippings, passages from dense novels about the Congo and word of mouth from real-life soldiers, sailors and nomads. A humanized internal version of the world was created within each person.

That was the way it was since before the time of Marco Polo to the time of Stanley and Livingston. Recently things have changed. Since the mid-sixties, when the saddle was firmly seated on the horse called TV, our notion of the world has been transformed. The world isn't "out there" anymore; instead: "We are the world." We float in a matrix of billions of image fragments, sound bites, plot-lines, news reports and ad copy. An endless stream of voices speaks to us—day in, day out, week in, week out.

Add to this the avalanche of *attitude* from every direction: comedians, talk shows, hit songs, interviews, speeches, reports, "specials" and on and on and on. The "cult of personality" has fragmented and dispersed as the Stalins and Hitlers have fallen, leaving us with thousands of mini-gods: stars, celebrities and "personalities." A world of information swirls around us, leaving us more knowledgeable about O.J. Simpson's housemates than our neighbors down the street.

The collage has become a whirling mobile of psyche and collective memory. One's own memory is the memory of millions of others, shared through the media. The "world" is no longer real and inaccessible; instead it is a surreal dimension from which escape is impossible. Millions think together and dream together. Slowly but surely, millions go mad together.

At the end of the day, the quesion "What do you think?" is almost impossible to answer. Thinking is no longer in any way linear, because knowledge is overwhelmed with incessant

details. Thoughts don't come; instead: "white noise." The bar-
rage of information layers and crowds itself into blather. No
resolution, only confusion.

In the midst of all of this is a life. My life. And I've got to
live my life. I've got to make choices. Most of these choices
and actions affect me directly: "What do I want to do today?"
"How should I raise my kids?" "How should I do my work?"
Some affect the world beyond me: "Am I 'for' universal health
coverage?" "Should I drink and drive?"

I am what I think, because my thinking affects my doing.
And my thinking is very, very noisy. Too much information.
"Should I give that bum a quarter?" "Should I perform in a
benefit?" "Should I eat margarine?" "Should I give a shit
about anything?"

I have plenty of facts. More facts than ever before.
Hundreds of inequities and sorrows crowd my mental hori-
zon daily via the "news": AIDS wards in New York; Mexican
peasant children's lack of schooling; the extinction of frogs
due to a thinning ozone layer; the suicidal tendencies of
American youth. Broccoli's anti-carcinogenic properties.

So I want to think a clear thought.

I'm trying to do that in *Pounding Nails in the Floor with My
Forehead*. I'm pounding out that shit, shaking it up, turning it
around. Right in front of a big bunch of people—an audience.
Everything goes into the pot: everything I think about; the
way I act; the way others act; the way people act on TV and
in movies; the way I act in front of the live audience at that
moment. It's a modern dance piece made of the collisions in
my mind. I'm figuring some kind of truth will emerge.

When I improvise, when I start to build a solo, I try to leave
the editorial side of my mind out of it. I try to let the words
flow from within, I let the piece define itself. It becomes a

kind of "automatic writing," telling me what's on my mind. *Pounding* is the fifth full solo in a series (*Men Inside, FunHouse, Drinking in America* and *Sex, Drugs, Rock & Roll* being the earlier ones) and like the others, it has a kind of theme built out of more basic drives. So tales of fear, greed, loneliness, power-mongering, etc., hook up with one another in each solo to become meditations on "getting high" or "responsibility" or, in the case of this show, "frustration."

But no matter how frustrated I get, if I can say it, if I do it in front of an audience, I get some relief. In other words, theater keeps me sane. For me, it is medicine for a toxic environment of electronic media mind-pollution. All that machine/profit-oriented info is poisonous to my inner machinery.

Theater clears my head because it takes the subtextual brainwashing of the media madness and SHOUTS that subtext out loud. ("You are shit compared to the fabulous creatures out there in star-world." Or "You are ineffectual because the world is too big for you to make a difference." Or "The solution to your misery is money, money, money!!!" Etc.) Somehow, when I really examine the boogeyman of my inner thoughts, he's not so scary. ("You are going to lose your job and end up homeless. Toe the line. Toe the line. Toe the line.")

Theater is ritual. It is something we make together every time it happens. Theater is holy. Instead of being bombarded by a cathode ray tube, we are speaking to ourselves. Human language, not electronic noise. Theater is laughter, which is always a valuable commodity.

Above all, theater is empathy as opposed to voyeurism. All good theater is about imagining a walk in someone else's shoes. And all theater asks the same question: What would I do if that were *me* up there?

I'm pretty sure about all of this. What I don't know, I put in my shows. There's alot I'm confused about. But one thing I know: Theater remains at the frontier of the greatest mystery—what it means to be human.

ACKNOWLEDGEMENTS

Lots of people to thank. First of all, my director, Jo, who fol-
lowed the show through every stage of production. Also
thanks to the theaters where *Pounding* lived before coming
to the Minetta Lane Theatre: P.S. 122 in New York, the
American Repertory Theatre in Cambridge, Mass., the
Almeida Theatre, London and the Mark Taper Forum in Los
Angeles. Thanks to Mark Russell, Dominick Balletta, Robert
Brustein, Rob Orchard, Michael Morris and Gordon
Davidson for their warm support.

Also special thanks to Edith Meeks, Philip Rinaldi, Jan
Kroeze, John Arnone, Kathy Haberthur, Roy Gabay and my
producers: Ron, Nick, Randy and Fred. Thanks to all the
superb staff at the Minetta Lane, particularly Robbie Young,
Mike Tkach and Robert Easter for their great sense of humor.

Finally, thanks to Terry Nemeth and Steve Samuels at TCG
for their care and guidance.

POUNDING NAILS
IN THE FLOOR WITH MY FOREHEAD

Pounding Nails in the Floor with my Forehead opened February 3, 1994 at the Minetta Lane Theatre, New York. Directed by Jo Bonney. Produced by Frederick Zollo, Nick Paleologus, Ron Kastner and Randy Finch.

A silhouette against the back wall of the theater reveals a man speaking into a microphone. We hear a basso profundo radio voice a la Rush Limbaugh.

I was shaving this morning. Shaving with a disposable razor and suddenly I thought of my *Dad.* I wondered, "What would I be doing right now, if it were forty years ago? If it wasn't 1994, but 1954 and I'm my own Dad?" And I imagined myself going downstairs, and there's my wife and she's not racing to meet the *car pool, no,* she's making me *breakfast.* She's got a gingham apron on, she's making me bacon and eggs . . . which I eat with tremendous pleasure because I've never even *heard* of cholesterol before.

And here are my children sitting at my 1954 breakfast table and they're well-behaved and well-dressed. In fact, my son is wearing a *necktie. I'm* wearing a necktie. I pick up the morning newspaper—all the news is *good*: we've won the war in Korea, they've found a cure for polio, employment's up, housing's up, everybody's *happy*.

I own my own home, I own my own car (which I wash every single Saturday), I love my wife, I like baseball, I believe in the President, and I pray to God in a place called *church.* No drugs. No drugs *anywhere.* Only people doing drugs in 1954 are William Burroughs and Allen Ginsberg!

No one's *complaining.* We're not hearing about women's rights and homosexual *rights* and minorities' rights and immigrants' rights. No *victims.* No sexual *harassment.* No worries about the environment. The environment is just fine, thank you.

No therapists. No twelve-step groups. No marches on Washington. No homeless people. No *AIDS.* Just good old-fashioned values like honesty and hard work and bravery and fidelity. And that's *it.* It's America forty years ago. Everybody's working. Everybody's straight. Everybody's happy.

And I thought to myself, what a wonderful world that must have been, a world without problems. I would love to be there right *now.* And then I remembered a *terrible* nightmare I'd had last night.

Now lemme tell you about this nightmare: It's the middle of the night, I'm in bed, of course, who shows up in my bedroom but *Bill Clinton.* As I said, it's a nightmare. He takes my hand and he says, "Come with me." And we float out the window and into the night air, and down to the street and we drop into this open manhole.

And we're walking around in the sewers, Bill and I. I'm thinking, I never trusted this guy, where's he taking me?

We walk and we walk and we come to this big cave and in this cave there are all these people lying around on mattresses, smoking things: pot, crack, hashish, opium. Whatever these people smoke.

And through the haze, I see all these familiar faces! Oh, there's Whoopi Goldberg reading the *Communist Manifesto*. And there's Ralph Nader bitching about something. And Susan Sarandon and Tim Robbins leading a peace rally. And Roseanne Arnold having sex with Madonna. And Ice T and Ice Cube and Vanilla Ice and all the other pieces of ice and all the other *troublemakers* and *commies* and *lefties* and people with green hair and tattoos and goatees and rings through their noses and rings through their nipples and rings through their penises.

And some of them are marching around protesting something . . . there's another bunch of them counting their food stamps and *welfare checks*. Right in front of me a bunch of idiots are watching *Beavis and Butt-head* on MTV.

And I'm horrified. And I turned to Bill and I said, "Bill, where are we? I'm frightened." And he said, "Don't you know?" And I said, "No. Hell?" And he laughed and he said, "No, of course not! This isn't Hell. Look around you. Don't you recognize the place? This is America, 1994! Better get used to it."

Let's go to a commercial.

Man emerges from darkness, coughing, scratching his balls, picking his butt and ranting.

Good afternoon ladies and gentlemens, homeboys and homeless, welcome to the soul train. We be making all local stops including fear, insanity, incarceration and death. Cigar, cigarette smoking is not permitted on my train, but if you got your stems, BEAM ME UP SCOTTY! HAHHHHHHH!

   I'm coming to Brooklyn, I'm coming to Queens, I'm coming to Manhattan!

(Faces the audience)

I am your *worst nightmare!* I got shit in my pants, I got fleas in my beard, I got so much syf-liss and gonorrhea pouring outta my penis, you can turn it on and off like a *faucet.*

(Arms flailing)

I am an exploding SUPERNOVA of negative energy. I am a cosmic comet moving through space, spewing my essence wherever I goes!

Hey sister. How you doing today? How you doing? This is my train, you know this is my subway train? It is! I'm the captain of this train. Where you going? You going to work? That's good. Nothing wrong with work, baby, get your ass on to work. . . . See that strap you hanging from, baby? I *sneezed* all over that strap jus' this morning. I did. You too, have a nice day.

Yo, homeboy! How you doing today? Watch out for that door you leaning against. Watch out! I threw up all over that door jus' last week. I did. Chicken pot pie. Was good. You dig around in those cracks and the crevices, you welcome to all the peas and carrots you can find.

See this seat here? This is my seat. This is my favorite seat in the whole train. Right in the middle so I can see both ends. I's sitting in this seat jus' yesterday. Jus' yesterday. Got all nice and comferble. I got so nice and comferble, I wet my pants.

That pee went running down through my curly hairs, down through my crusty underwears, made a little puddle. Made kind of a soup out of myself. Hah! Got all the ingredients right there, stuck on me. Smear of dog food left over from breakfast. Some rat blood from some rat I stomped. Some Chinaman's snot, they don't give you no respect, you're lying on the ground, *(Mimes blowing nose)* hit you when you're trying to get some *rest.* All that stuff boils together, make a soup.

I sat in that soup for awhile then it got all cold. Then I wasn't comferble no more.

So I got up, went down the other end of the train. It's alright, it's alright.

(Indicates seat)

It dries. It dries. All's left on the seat were some molecules. Can't even see 'em.

Know you can't see 'em, 'cause a guy came on the train, Frank, Frank the businessman in his camel's hair coat and his briefcase, came on the train, sat right down in those molecules, didn't bother him in the least.

He was rushing home, had to rush home 'cause he's got to see the evening *news*, find out what's going on in the world. He can't see with his own eyes, he's gotta see it on the TV set.

Go home to his condominium. Walked in the door, threw his camel's hair coat on the couch and said, "HONEY, I'M HOME!" That's what they say those suburbs people, gots to let everyone know where they are at. "Honey, I'm home." "Honey, I'm going out for five minutes." "Honey, I'm back!" Who gives a shit where he is?

Frank sat down, ate his dinner. Yum!

And then Frank stood up and said, "Honey! That was delicious! That was the best roast duck I had all week. Hey, honey! Guess what I did at work today? I fired a hundred and fifty motherfuckers! My dick is ten feet long, I'm feeling sexy, let's fuck!"

And then he grabbed his wife, who has a beautiful body 'cause she's on the Stairmaster three hours a day and drug her into the living room and threw her right on the couch. And they proceeded to have some really really good sex.

That's 'cause they got this video called "How to Have Really Really Good Sex." And they did it every which way, up and down all around. The one-legged position. Doggie style. Handstands.

And they be bouncing up and down on that couch. And the camel's hair coat be bouncing up and down on that couch. And all my *molecules* they be bouncing up and down, right along with 'em.

And then Frank decided to do something he hadn't done in a long time. He took his wife's legs and he spread 'em like this and he took the tip of his tongue, he's gonna put that tongue right on his wife's vagino. Don't ask me why.

But just as the tip of his tongue was going to touch those wet curly hairs, just as it was going to touch, shwoop, one a my molecules went right down his throat!

He didn't feel it. Didn't feel a thing. *But he will.* 'Cause my shit's strong. And those molecules gonna bubble and boil, gonna mutate and grow down there deep inside of Frank. Gonna make a change in Frank. Gonna change his *lifestyle.*

Those molecules, they gonna start spinning inside Frank's brain. He's gonna start doing shit he never done before. He's gonna get himself some bulletproof underwear. He's gonna start sterilizing his water. Get his wife checked for HIV, his kids checked for HIV, his Granma checked for HIV. He's gonna start looking over his shoulder when he walks down the street.

He's gonna put radar on his roof. He's gonna put extra alarms on his car, extra locks on his doors.

He's not gonna let his kids out to play. He's not gonna answer his phone, he's not gonna get the mail. He's gonna get himself some dark glasses, stay inside the house, never go out.

And then he's gonna get himself a gun. And then he's gonna wait. First person knocks on his door: BOOM, he's gonna shoot him.

See 'cause Frank's been infected. He's infected with the dis-ease. The disease of *fear*. And that fear's gonna eat him right up from asshole to brain. And those molecules, when they done with Frank, gonna jump off to the next guy.

(Pointing around the audience)

To the next guy, the next guy, the next guy, the next guy.

'Cause we all infected see? 'Cause we all on the *same train*. And nobody gets off this train. Nobody gets off this train.

And I'm the Captain of this train. I'M THE CAPTAIN OF THIS TRAIN!

So I say: fasten your seat belts, ladies and gentlemen, hang onto your straps. 'Cause like it or not, me and my molecules are about to take everybody here for a nice long ride!

After the last piece, "Molecules," the audience has applauded weakly or not at all. Pick up a hand mic and address the audience.

Thank you.

(Some people clap, if none clapped before)

No, no, it's too late. But thank you. I'm very happy you could all make it tonight. It really means alot to me. Means alot to all of us, I'm sure. Or maybe not, maybe it doesn't mean anything, I don't know.

But thanks anyway. It's great that you're all, uh, sitting out there and I'm standing up here and you're all, uh, you know, looking at me. I like to be looked at so uh thank you. You're doing just what I want you to do. Just sit back, relax, put on your glasses, get out your binoculars, focus your telescopes 'cause here I am.

And I want to thank you for this opportunity to reveal

myself. Expose myself. Strip naked, so to speak. Take it off. Take it all off. Really show you everything I can be.

Which isn't much, I know. I mean, if you're disappointed, I understand. I've never really been a likeable person. In fact I'm kind of an unlikable person. And, you know, maybe you're a *likeable* person, so maybe you feel *superior* to me because you're easy to get along with and I'm not.

I don't really care what you think.

But, so, uh, is everybody ready to have a good time? Just went out and had something to eat in the neighborhood? Maybe a little nouvelle cuisine before the show?

(Addresses someone in the front row)

Maybe a little wilted radicchio salad with a honey mustard vinaigrette? Would you like some fresh pepper with that sir? We have a very nice chardonnay. A very *nice* chardonnay. Would you like to hear today's specials?

No. How 'bout the balcony? Something ethnic before you came by tonight? Something Third World? A little cous-cous, maybe, tandori, fajita, burrito? Nothing like a nice hot ethnic dish before you go to see that semi-expensive, semi-meaningful Off-Broadway show. Nothing like a nice hot dish from a country where no one can actually *afford* to eat the very thing you're stuffing your face with. Waiter probably had rickets when he was a kid. "Here you go sir . . . oh, thank you, a penny tip! I'm so happy now!"

Did you have some nice Third World beer with your burritos? Maybe some DOS EQUIS? Six pack of Dos Equis? Down front here, a couple of bottles of chardonnay. Couple of hits of acid in the back row?

I don't care what you do with your free time. You come in

here and you're just so comfortable and so easygoing and likeable and you're just such a nice person. And you come in here and you've got this *attitude*. No, no. I know the attitude. You don't even clap when I kill myself on the first bit. You judge me. You sit there and you *judge* me. Don't act like I can't see you, I can see you.

(Mimic an audience member whispering to her neighbor)

"What is this? Why did you bring me to this? No, there are no nails up there, Sid, he's not going to pound anything! I'm telling you: Phyllis came last week. She says all he does is play *assholes*. I have enough assholes in my life already, who needs one more?"

Well you know what? Who needs *you*? You're just taking up a seat. You don't think I'm so great? I don't think you're so great either. So we're even.

I mean, you come in here, you make no effort at all. I'm supposed to jump all over the place, like some kind of puppet on a string, *entertain* you! Hey, let's get something straight, in case you don't know what you just paid thirty-five bucks to see, this is what I do. This is my work. This is my life up here. OK? This isn't *Ace Ventura, Pet Armenian*!

(Hits the floor)

You don't like it, fine with me. Fine with fucking me.

(Moves offstage, into the wings)

It's OK, it's OK, I'm not angry. "He's angry! He's got an angry social message. He's the cutting edge of the black hole of the American psyche! I read about it in the *Village Voice*!

(Returning)

Fuck that shit! I'm not angry, OK? I'm happy.

Because I know that being unhappy and angry and pessimistic is a big turn-off. You didn't come here tonight to hear alot of pessimistic, negative stuff. You came here tonight to be entertained, to be uplifted, to build up an appetite for the decaf cappuccino after the show.

And I *want* you to like me, I want to have a warm loving relationship with this audience, I don't want to have a dysfunctional relationship to this audience. I want to bond with this audience.

By the end of the night I want us to be as one, like a giant school of fish swimming shoulder to shoulder with hundreds of thousands of compadres.

And we'll move together as one to make a greater dream possible! A world where love and harmony will rule, and everyone is happy and well fed and disease-free and PART OF.

I want to stand up here tonight and say: "I AM ONE AMONG MANY." I don't want to rock the boat, I want to help *row*!

That's what I want, and I know that's what you want too.

You know we've all been through alot of therapy over the past ten years, and I'm very proud of where my therapy has taken me. I learned some things. And the cornerstone of what I've learned can be said in three little words: "People are special."

You know I was in my apartment last week when that big snowstorm hit and I could see the first few snowflakes falling. And I didn't get all negative. I didn't think: "Oh shit another snowstorm." No. I watched those snowflakes falling, what was I watching, a hundred thousand, two hundred thousand snowflakes, and you know what I thought?

I thought: "Every one of those snowflakes is different. Unique." But you know what else? They're all the same, because they're all snow.

And that's what we are. Every one of us. Every person here tonight is unique, special . . . but every person here is exactly the same. Every person here has a skull in their head, blood in their veins. Take a straight razor, run it across your wrist, every person here bleeds.

We just have our particular loves and hates, likes and dislikes. That's what makes each of us different.

(Look at audience member)

You. You like Mariah Carey. Now, I, I hate Mariah Carey. So in that way, we're different.

(Another audience member)

You think Phil Collins is a genius? Phil Collins makes me puke.

(To the balcony)

Up in the balcony: you love Pearl Jam. Every time I listen to them I think: "What the fuck does 'Pearl Jam' mean? What does it mean???!!!"

You want to know what I like? I like the sound of a jackhammer ripping concrete at six o'clock in the morning outside my bedroom window. I like the sound of a dentist's drill. I like the sound of the dial tone, real loud. I like the sound of two cats fucking. I like the sound of an eighty-year-old grandmother taking out her dentures at night.

I like the announcements they make in the subways:

(Speak into the mic in garbled gibberish)

What do you like? Do you like it alot? Have you given it alot of thought? I hope so. I really hope so. Because I'll tell you something right now, you take everybody in this room and strip all of you naked and shave your heads, stick you in a tiny little cell, feed you one watery bowl of gruel a day and you know what? IT WOULDN'T MAKE A FLYING FUCK WHAT YOU LIKE!

So thank you . . . thanks alot for coming . . . thank you. I hope you like the show.

Stride out onto the stage, arms stretched out, to applause. In a mild Southern accent.

Thank you! Thank you so much! I am so *happy* to see so many happy, smiling faces in this audience here tonight. I am *turned on* by the potential for change I feel in this room. I can feel it coming up out of the audience, into my legs, my body, my head. I am *exploding* with the power of change in this room tonight!

You know, I go all over this great country of ours, talking to audiences just like you, about change, about human potential. And everywhere I go, people ask me the same question, they say, "Phil . . . what is the secret of happiness? What is the secret of joy? Of ecstasy?"

And everywhere I go, I tell people the same story. I tell them a story about a little boy who went into a candy store and all he had was a nickel. He went into that store and he picked out the candy bar he wanted more than any other.

And he said to the man behind the counter, "Sir, I would like that candy bar right there. Here is my nickel."

And the man looked down at the little boy and the little boy's nickel and he said, "Son, that is a ten-cent candy bar. I'm sorry, I can't sell it to you." And the boy was disappointed by this news. But he thought and he thought and he thought and he came up with an *idea*. He said, "Why don't we *compromise*? I'll give you my nickel. We can take that candy bar, cut it in half. I'll have half, you have half for yourself. How 'bout that?"

And the man said to the little boy, "Son, that is a ten-cent candy bar. Get your skinny ass out of my store. Get yourself another nickel and I will sell it to you." And with that the man turned his back on the little boy.

And the little boy felt terribly rejected and cut off and abandoned. And he looked up at the man's broad back and he looked at the nickel in his hand and then he looked at the candy bar he wanted *so much*. And he reached out and *touched* the candy bar. And then he reached out and he *held* the candy bar. And then he ran out the store with the candy bar.

And as he was running down the street, he realized something: He still had his nickel in his hand! And in his other hand he had a *whole* candy bar! And he was suddenly filled with a tremendous feeling of *happiness* and *joy* and *ecstasy*.

Now let me ask you something: When was the last time you felt that good? I bet you can't even remember.

You wanna know something? I feel that good every day. I feel that good every day because I am in touch with something deep inside of me. And I'm going to show you how to get in touch with the same thing deep inside of you.

You see, a few years ago I was in a very bad place in my life. Like most of you here tonight I was severely depressed,

I was virtually suicidal. And I had to do some serious soul-searching.

One day, I was searching around in my soul, and I heard a little voice behind me. It said: "Hi Phil, remember me?" And I turned around (I was in my soul of course), and there on the floor of my soul was a *little tiny baby*. I had discovered my *inner baby within*!

You see, I have a baby inside of me and that baby needs to be picked up. That baby needs to be coddled. That baby needs to have things go its own way once in awhile. It needs to cry. It needs to piss on people, it has to throw up on people. That's my inner baby within.

And the miracle is, every single one of us here has a little tiny inner baby inside of him or her. I don't care how old, or ugly, perverse or disturbed you might be, you were once a sweet, little, adorable, happy little baby. That baby is inside you right now.

That baby is talking to you, but you're not listening. Let's listen to our babies for a moment. Let's listen to my baby. What's my baby saying? "Mommy." Hear that? "Daddy." "Barney." My baby wants to get out, watch some TV!

Come on now, I want everybody to reach down and pick up his or her little baby. Go ahead, don't be afraid! Put your baby on your lap. And I want you to think about little babies.

Ever watch a happy baby playing? They don't worry about tomorrow, they don't worry about yesterday. They don't worry about hurting other people's feelings. They don't worry about being responsible on the job or driving too fast or smoking too much. They don't read the newspaper, they don't watch the news, and they don't obey the law. Babies are in the NOW, they are connected to their centers. Babies are rude, they are crude, they are selfish, and they are *happy*.

And what do we do to these perfect little happy human beings? We take them and we make them into adults, don't we?

(Mimes building wall around the baby)

We build a wall around our inner baby made of fear and anxiety and negativity and responsibility and hatred. Brick by brick, we build that wall: jealousy and guilt and ambition. Shame, lots of shame, let's get that shame up there. Brick by brick we wall them in around and around until our inner baby is trapped *(Miming trapped)* like a miniature Marcel Marceau!

I'm telling you to tear down that wall and let that baby out! Come on now and let your baby go!

Get rid of that negativity. Stop worrying about tomorrow, stop worrying about yesterday! Stop worrying about what everybody else thinks about you all the time, what people think about you is none of your business! Stop worrying all the time. It's not helping anything! Sure there are people who are miserable all over the world, but hell, being all pissy and negative isn't going to do them much good, now is it? Sure the world is a complicated place, trying to understand it isn't going to make it any less complicated! Let me tell you something, the world has existed for twenty million years without your help, and it's gonna keep on going with or without you. Stop worrying about the whales and the elephants. They don't need you, your baby needs you!

I want you to take your baby's hand, go ahead, take it, it's not very big. And let that baby lead you to a new life of happiness, joy, and *healthy selfishness*!

From this day onward you're gonna get up every morning

and look into the mirror . . . you're gonna look into the mirror, you're gonna say to yourself: What . . . about . . . *ME?* When's it gonna be my turn? What about my *baby?*

You get in late for work. You're fifteen minutes late, the boss is pissed off. TOO BAD! FUCK YOU! My baby needed the sleep.

You forgot to send your Mom a Mother's Day card? She'll just have to wait till next year. Sorry, Mom. I'm busy being the mother you never were!

Driving around for half an hour trying to find someplace to park. Only parking spot is one of those handicapped parking spaces. You *park* there, your inner baby is handicapped!

It's midnight, you're watching Letterman on TV, halfway through that pint of Häagen Dazs, you finish it up, your baby needs that *nurturing.* Have another one! Chase it with a couple of Slim-Jims. Your baby needs your love!

You're gonna take care of your inner baby and this isn't going to be some part-time thing! You're going to be thinking about your inner baby incessantly. You're gonna be going to inner baby groups, talking to other inner babies on the phone. You're gonna buy videotapes, you're gonna buy my audiotapes, you're gonna read my books. I'm gonna sell you a little yellow sign, you put it in the window of your car, it's gonna say: "Caution, Inner Baby Within!"

You're gonna make your inner baby happy and when you do, you make yourself happy and when you're happy there will be one more happy person in the world. And you know what?

You will have made the world a better place.

OK, we're gonna break up into groups now and I'm gonna come around and talk to each of your inner babies, individually.

Picks up a glass of water, drinks, puts the glass down and addresses the audience.

You know what they say: "The glass is half empty or the glass is half full." That's pretty much my philosophy of life. You're born, you live, you *die.* And somewhere along the line, glass is going to be empty or glass is gonna be full. Empty, full, empty, full, empty, full, empty, full.

I remember when *I* was a little baby, glass was definitely on the empty side. I didn't have much going for me when I was born. I was only about this big, very small, only weighed about seven pounds. Naked. Crying. Bald. Life was full of challenges: learn to walk, learn to talk, use a spoon, tie my shoe, wipe my ass. *One thing after the next thing after the next after the next thing after the next!*

I mean I'm just this little baby and they cut me *no* slack. Then it's: "Get out of the house." Kindergarten, high school, college. I mean it's the same for everybody, right? Learn to drive, get a job, find a place to live, find a love. It's exhausting.

And basically what happens is one day you find yourself in a store buying a TV set and you realize you've arrived, you're all grown up. You're an adult now. Glass is finally half-full. Here's your TV, go home and watch it.

And then you have to make it in this world and if you have any luck at all, you have some modicum of success and then you get to do all these adult things. You get to have a credit card: "Here's your credit card." Get to go on vacation packages, have a barbecue now and then and um . . . what else? A bigger TV with a remote control, give you a little power in your life.

Get to be condescending to people younger than you. Get to enter the Publishers Clearing House contests, subscribe to lots and lots of stuff you don't really need, trying to put some hope in your life. But all you end up with is stacks of glossy magazines all over your house with little perfume inserts in them that you peel apart so you can sniff the sweet smell of success and remain completely frustrated.

And you do this. You do this for about twenty-five or thirty years and then one day you look in the mirror and you realize your hair's getting a little thin and your stomach's not as flat as it used to be and your dick isn't as hard as it used to be. And from that day on all you can think about is how your hair is falling, your stomach's drooping, your dick is limping.

And basically it just gets worse and worse and worse until you're incontinent, mindless and drooling, stuck in a wheel-chair in some firetrap senior citizens home next to an inter-state highway. And your big thrill of the day is when they're serving strained peaches.

You're sitting in your wheelchair, strapped in so you don't fall over, you're listening to the sound of the traffic whizzing by out on the highway. Maybe you're counting the cars: "Two thousand one, two thousand two, two thousand three." And the attendant brings lunch, which you don't really like, but you like the strained peaches.

And there's this moment, just as that fragment of peach runs down over your old cracked tongue, and for that one moment, for that two or three seconds, everything is good again. Hope is in the air, the glass is half-full once more.

But then you start coughing and gagging 'cause you don't have any teeth, you're not that good at swallowing anymore, and the attendant is shouting in your one good ear, "Come on! Come on! You can do better than that! That's no attitude to take!" as you shit your pants for the fourth time that day. And think to yourself, if you're capable of thinking anything at all: "DOES DOCTOR KEVORKIAN WORK IN THIS PLACE? I WANT DOCTOR KEVORKIAN!!!"

But that's all kind of in the future for me. I'm pretty happy, things are good.

It can be a beautiful day like today and I can step out into the day and I can think to myself: "This is good." But even if it *is* a perfect day and the birds are singing and the sky is blue and I'm holding my four-year-old's hand and everything is perfect, in a way it isn't, because *somewhere*, and I am reminded of this constantly on the evening news, somebody is suffering like you would not *fucking believe*!

I mean right now as I say these words, somewhere in Africa, there is a vast sea of human beings slowly starving to death! A sea of human skeletons *dying*. They're standing under the same blue sky, the same sun, they're holding their children's hands too.

What can they be thinking as they look down at their kids' bony heads and ribby ribcages and bulging bellies and big brown eyes full of death flies? What can they possibly be thinking? *(African voice)* "Oh well, the glass is half-empty or the glass is half-full?" Yeah. *Right.*

STARVING AFRICANS, STARVING AFRICANS, STARVING AFRICANS, STARVING AFRICANS, STARVING AFRICANS! They spoil everything!

I mean, wait a second. I'd love to help them. And I try, I send them money. But, I can't *fix* them. I don't even really know where they are. Where are they? Does anybody here know where they are? You don't know where they are. *I* know where they are. They're on my TV set, every night, 6:30 PM, channel 2.

It all gets very confusing and depressing. And when I get confused and depressed, what I do, I get in my car, I go to the supermarket, I grab a cart and push it around.

I don't know, something about the supermarket makes me feel better. The environment is so clean and orderly—air-conditioned. I mean the name says it all: SUPERMARKET. It's like where Superman goes to shop. And that's the way I feel, as I push my cart around, my cape flying behind me, grabbing that bottled water from a melted glacier ("Oh, only five dollars a quart! That's reasonable!"), the mesquite charcoal chips, double-A alkaline batteries for the kids' toys. Blue Jamaican coffee beans from some blue Jamaican! "Oh! Strained peaches on sale! Never know when I might need some of those!"

I keep going until I fill up my cart, then I know I'm finished. I push my cart to the check-out counter, I am reaffirmed in my right to exist in this environment, because I have the *cash*. This stuff costs alot of money and I've got it. Makes me feel good. And as I pass the cash over to the checkout girl, it's almost a sexual thing. It's like I am inseminating her with my worth. I want to say to her: "See, I can pay for it! I got it up! Now, check it out!"

And as I carry my bags of groceries out to my freshly waxed and detailed automobile sitting in the middle of the parking lot, I'm not confused and depressed anymore. It all makes sense now. I'm serene again . . . because, because I feel deep down, I deserve this good life. I work so hard. I work hard at my job, I work hard at my marriage, I work out hard at the gym, I work hard at raising my kids. I MAKE AN EFFORT. I wear sun-block when it's sunny out. I floss my teeth every day. I recycle!

I'm a team player and I play by the rules: Pay the charge cards on time, change my oil every three thousand miles, don't drink when driving. No binging, no drug-taking, no wife-swapping, no four-in-the-morning-one-more-shot-of-vodka drinking, no speeding, no yelling, no spitting, no cursing, no dancing, no running. Just say "no."

That's my life: "Just say no."

You're either on the bus or you're off the bus. But you gotta know the rules: Don't black out, don't shoot up, don't go down on strange pussy.

Wear a condom on everything: dick, tongue, eyes, nose, fingers, rectum and brain. Remember your social security number and don't disappear. Don't go to India for a year, don't hitchhike down Highway 61, don't walk on the wild side, don't leave your job or you may find the bus has left without you.

And in exchange for all this good behavior I get a brand

new car with a factory installed mobile phone. And I can drive my car and talk on the phone and it feels good. I feel like I really belong.

I can come to a stop sign and be blabbing on the phone for three bucks a minute and there's a guy picking bottles out of a trash can for a nickel apiece and it's OK. It's OK. 'Cause I'm doing the best I can, and I know he's doing the best *he* can.

I want to roll down the window of the car and throw that guy a buck and say: "I'm there for you man, I'm there for you. When the revolution comes, I am on *your* side."

Because I am on his side. I'm one of the good guys! I give money to every charity, I wear my red ribbon, I lick stamps for the benefit committee. I have the t-shirts and the tote bags and the coffee mugs to prove my commitment.

I read the morning paper every day, I watch the evening news every night. Lot of painful stories on that news. And I am there for those people. I am there for their pain. "SHOW ME YOUR PAIN, I AM THERE FOR YOU!"

And because I know that I care, I know that I am concerned, my glass isn't just half-full, it's overflowing! Because I love. Love is in my life. I love my wife and kids, I love all of you here tonight, I love every single person in the whole world—every single person in Africa, in Asia, in South America. I wish they were all here right now so I could hug them.

My glass is overflowing because the glass is the glass of life and it is filled with love. And I am drinking with relish from my glass of life. And that love is going down my throat, into my body and it fills my soul. And I drink and I drink, and after awhile I drink so much my bladder gets kind of full and I have to pee. And I pee love. I'm drinking, I'm peeing. I'm drinking and peeing love at the same time.

And oh, here comes that guy from the trash can with his bottle and he needs some love too! Well I've got plenty of love to spare. Bring that bottle over here, dude. Let's fill that right up. And here comes somebody from Zaire with a little tin can and that guy pisses into the Zaire guy's can. And here's somebody from Haiti, and somebody from the slums of Rio! We're all drinking and pissing and drinking and pissing and everybody is giving love to everybody else and that's the way the world goes round.

I'm doing the best I can.

Look, a hundred years from now I will just be some bones in a box and so will you and so will that guy picking out the bottles. So what I did in this puny little life of mine will not have made much difference.

But I will tell you one thing. While I was on this earth, I lived and I loved . . . and I was concerned. And that's what's important.

I am concerned therefore I am.

RED

Cross stage, grab a beer bottle, shout off in a gruff voice.

Come on up, man, come on up. Don't worry, dogs won't bite ya, they won't bite ya, 'less I tell 'em to. Just come up the stairs. HARLEY! DAVIDSON! Sit! Come on in, man. Sit down, sit down. You wanna beer?

(Shouts off)

RAINBOW! RAINBOW! Get my friend a beer here, please! What's your name again? Richard.

(To "Rainbow")

GET RICHARD A BEER! THANK YOU.

(Reaches into t-shirt pocket)

Here man, check this out. Hawaiian sensimilla. Seven fifty for the quarter ounce. Excellent, excellent weed. Two tokes of this, you forget how to jerk off.

(To "Rainbow")

Rainbow! Come on! Help me out here, I'm working. I don't want to leave this guy alone with the dogs!

She's a stripper so she thinks she's better than other people.

What do you do, man? Wait, lemme guess, I'm good at this . . . a . . . Federal narcotics agent! Hah-hah. No, no, wait a second—Armani suit, Rolex watch, shifty eyes. You're a stockbroker. Right?

I always get it, 'cause I deal to alot a people, make alot a money. You'd be surprised who I deal to. Nothing wrong with making money, nothing wrong with money, as long as you know how to spend it.

I know some people, they make all this money, they waste it on like expensive cars, expensive boats, houses. They waste it on their kids. Kids' college education. What's the point of making all this money if you're not going to enjoy it, if you're not going to use it to either get fucked-up or get fucked, you know what I mean?

I know this one guy, stockbroker like you, he's into skiing. Flies all around the world, skis in all these weird places. Spends like $50,000 a year on skiing. Takes helicopters to the top of mountains so he can, you know, ski where nobody ever skied before.

Hey, I been skiing, man, skiing's cool. You go up the hill, you come down the hill, you go up the hill, you come down the hill, you go up the hill, you get cold, you come down the hill, you break your leg. It's a *goof.*

But, like, how can you compare that with like getting together with your old lady on a Saturday night, rolling up some fat doobs of some fine Jamaican shit, get nicely toasted, put some mellow music on the stereo, ZZ Top, Motorhead, whatever.

You start dancing around, screwing around. You're licking each other, you're sucking each other, next thing you know, you're humping like a couple of happy puppies. All of a sudden, BOOM, you spill your load. You're lying on the bed and you feel fucking amazing. You feel like Jesus Christ resurrected.

Why? Why do you feel so good? Because . . . you're *stoned* and you just had an *orgasm*, right? Simple arithmetic. It's like the pinnacle of human experience.

You know what I'm saying, man? I mean, isn't that the best feeling in the whole world? Don't you love that feeling? I love that feeling.

You're lying on the bed, the two of yas, you're all spaced out. All sweaty and smelly, you smell like a couple of camels at the zoo. You got stuff all stuck all over ya. Your hair's all pushed over to one side. She's lying there, she's got a big puddle of come on her belly. And you're like writing your name in the come. And then you start fooling with her honey pot.

And she's like OHHHHHH! And then she reaches and starts yanking on your joystick and the two of you are like OOOOOHHHH!! AAAHHHHHH! Next thing you know: "Oh, look who's back in action, the little soldier!"

So you get ready to do it again, because the second time's always the best, you know what I mean? Always the best. And you get ready to stick it in . . .

But what do you gotta do before you stick it in? What do you *always* haveta do?

Get out the hash pipe, right?

One hit on the hash pipe. Toss some coke on her tits, lick it up. And then you slide it in nice and slow. You stick her toes in your ears, she sticks her thumb up your asshole. You grab her ass, she grabs your butt. She's screaming, you're barking . . . OH OH OH OH OH! BOOOOOOM and you come so hard you feel like you're gonna be brain-damaged for the rest of your life, and you fall back onto the bed but just before your head hits the pillow you grab that bottle of tequila, take one last snort and your brain does a slow dive into a black hole of complete and utter *satisfaction.*

(Tokes, thinks)

I mean, how can you compare that with skiing, man? You know?

Good pot, huh, man? You got some drool hanging down off your lip there, better wipe it off.

Here try this coke. It just came in, haven't put a cut on it yet. No charge, no charge. Come on, man, *party* with me. You only live once!

Here lemme cut you a line.

(Mime cutting a long line on the table. Pause)

Actually, I'll do that one.

(Snorts up the line)

ROCK & ROLL! People just don't know how to relax anymore!

I was watching TV last night and this commercial comes on . . .

Go ahead, man, knock yourself out, I got three keys in the back you finish that.

This commercial comes on these two people are drinking cups of coffee, and they're going like: "Oh, I love to relax with a cup of coffee."

Who the hell relaxes with coffee? Serial killers, that's who. I hear Ted Bundy was a big coffee drinker.

I mean what's with this coffee thing? Cappuccino, expresso! Everywhere I go now there's these little places where people are sitting around sucking down this black shit! Get themselves all wired up then they hook themselves up to their car phones and their beepers and their fax machines and they're like . . . AAAAAAHHHHH!

I mean why does everybody need a car phone all of a sudden? I remember when the only guys who had car phones were cops. Like for emergencies. What's the big emergency, everyone has to have a car phone?

(Picks up imaginary phone)

DON'T FORGET TO PICK UP THE COFFEE ON YOUR WAY HOME!!!

(To "Rainbow")

RAINBOW BABY, COME ON BRING OUT THOSE BEERS! THIS GUY'S GRINDING HIS TEETH SO HARD I'M GETTING A HEADACHE!

She's great, wait till you meet her, man. She's very talented. We should go see her show. You like nipples, labia? She's got all that stuff, man. We'll go see her, you and me.

See, you're normal, man, you're a normal human being.

The people out there, man, they're so psycho, I'm afraid to go out of the house.

I go down the 7-Eleven last night to like pick up a little nightcap before I go to bed, right? So I'm walking out of the store with my three six packs, right? Minding my own business. And there's this guy sitting in his Mercedes, talking on his car phone. And he's like checking me out. So I check him out. So he checks me out again. So I check him out again. So he locks all the doors of his car.

I'm like, "Hey." You know? Walk up to his car. Pulled out my lizard, whizzed all over his hood ornament. Then I snapped it off and I ate it.

(Laughing)

Not really. Break ya teeth if you do that.

So anyway, I'm in this weird mood, so I get in my pickup, pop a cold one, turn on the radio. And my favorite song in the whole world is playing: "Give Peace a Chance." So I'm like rolling down the road, singing. You know?

All of a sudden this negative DJ comes on starts going on and on about the "tragedy of John Lennon." Bumming me completely out. And I'm thinking, what the fuck is the tragedy of John Lennon? I mean I know who John Lennon was, right? Guy was rich, he was famous, people thought he was God, he was a Beatle for crying out loud.

Went around the world about nine hundred times, had sex with everybody he wanted to have sex with, did more drugs than you can carry in an aircraft carrier, he did it all! One night, he's coming home from work and some asshole is waiting for him with a .38, BOOM, BOOM, BOOM, BOOM, BOOM!!

Like flipping off a light switch. That's it, finished. That's the way I want to go, man. Bullet straight to the heart, no warning. I mean we all go, right? Or did I make that up?

Shit, I left friends back in the 'Nam, they were still twitching the last time I saw 'em. Half his age. I got buddies in the AIDS ward, shooters, dying that long slow painful death. Fuck that shit.

Tragedy of John Lennon! My life should be half as tragic as that dude's. I could use some of that tragedy in *my* life.

You wanna know about tragedy? I'll tell you about tragedy. My best friend in the whole world, Kenny, man. Now that's a tragic story. Most righteous, courageous motherfucker I ever knew. Me and him were like this, man.

(Crosses fingers)

Used to deal drugs together. Washington Square Park, 1971. Used to deal to the hippies. Just soft drugs: pot, mescaline, psilocybin, acid. We used to get this acid, man, pure liquid LSD. Absolutely pure. You fill a syringe with this shit, stick it in your neck, you're tripping in five seconds. You'd love it, man, I know you'd love it.

We used to deal drugs all day long. And then at night, anything we didn't sell, we did it. It was like bungee jumping without the cord. Whoaaa!

Me and Kenny, we used to ride around on these big Harley hogs. And one day, we were stopped at this stop light and both had these two knapsacks full of psilocybin mushrooms strapped to our backs. We just looked at each other, didn't even say a word. At the exact same moment, we reached into our knapsacks, pulled out a handful of mushrooms, ate 'em, took off down the highway. Did not come back for three *years*, man.

Ended up in Loveland, Colorado. Ever been to Loveland, man? Nice in Loveland. Mountains and trees and shit. We used to just hang out in the mountains, tripping. Check 'em out. Try and figure out how much the mountains *weighed.*

So one night, we're up in the mountains and we've got this campfire going. And we're trying to roast this deer we had shot. And out of the blue, Kenny turns to me and says, "Red, will you promise me something?"

And I look him in the eyes and he's looking at me and I swear, man, I can see right down into his soul. And I say, "Sure, man, I'm your blood brother, man. I'll promise anything you want."

He says, "No listen, I'm serious, man." He says, "I'm in this really good place in my life, man, and I want you to promise me, if I ever fucking sell out, I want you to come find me, stick a shotgun in my mouth and pull the trigger." You know?

So anyway, long story short . . . Kenny was always gambling. And six years ago, he bought this lottery ticket and he won. Not much. A million bucks. After taxes, that's like five hundred thousand dollars. I'm thinking party time.

Kenny decides he wants to change his lifestyle. Cuts off his hair, shaves off his beard, goes back to school, learns to read. Meets this chick, gets married, they have a kid. Got a job, he's an engineer now, believe it or not. Lives in New Jersey in this big house, a swimming pool, a four-wheel drive and a lawn. The whole nine yards.

And I don't see him that much anymore because you know, he's busy with his shit, and I got my work and everything.

Last week he calls me up and says, "Red, I'm having this big barbecue up at the house, you wanna come up?" And I got this one principle, never miss a fucking party.

So me and Rain, we get on the hog, we hightail up to New Jersey. We show up, it's this big spread, all these people are there, people Kenny works with, his neighbors. And I'm cool with those people, I'm like: "Hello, how are you. Cheerio." All that shit.

So I see Kenny is like hanging out over by the pool talking to this guy, so I'm hanging with him, listening. And he's like . . . he's like explaining how the filter in the pool works and I'm like not hip to that shit, you know?

So like me and Rainbow had been doing 'ludes since about ten o'clock in the morning, so we're kind of in this festive mood. And anyway, I end up on top of this gazebo thing next to the pool, kind of naked. Well, actually, completely naked. And Rainbow's trying to squirt me with this water hose, trying to make me laugh and fall down, right?

So anyways, I fall down . . . crack my head on the cement, then I flip over into the pool. I'm like under water for a couple of minutes, finally I pull myself out, puke all over Kenny's boss.

Funny right? I mean it's a party, I'm partying.

Next thing I know, Kenny's all pissed off, throwing me outta the party, telling me I embarrassed him in front of his friends. And I looked into his eyes and . . . it wasn't Kenny anymore, Kenny was gone. And then I remembered what he made me promise him in Loveland, so now I gotta go down Florida next week and pick up a shotgun.

But I will do that for him, man, because I love him that much. I do. I made that promise.

(Thrusts his arm forward)

Check out this scar, man, a hundred and fifty-seven stitches. You know how I got that scar? I put my fist through a plate glass window. You know why I put my fist through that plate glass window? 'Cause it was there.

Check it out, man, *(Thumps his chest)* forty-five years old. You wanna know why I look so good? 'Cause I get fucked-up every fucking day. I'M FREE. LIVE FREE OR DIE. DON'T TREAD ON ME. I'M AN OUTLAW, MAN, DON'T EVER FUCKING FORGET IT.

(Stalks off, returns)

It's OK, man . . . I'm not pissed off at you. You're an outlaw too. It's like you're an inside outlaw and I'm an outside outlaw.

I like you, man, you like me, man? Good.

I love you, man, you love me, man?

You know, she's never gonna bring that beer. Fuck this pot and coke shit, you and me we should do something. We're getting solid. I can't let you go back to that rat wheel where you work.

You know what? I got a great idea, man! I still got some of that liquid LSD in the freezer. No, don't worry about it. You don't have to pay. You and me, man, let's go out and look over the edge, man. No. No. Listen, this is a great idea. Just sit there, man, I'll go get it.

Just sit there, don't move. You don't move, the dogs won't bite ya. I'll be right back. I just gotta go get the syringes.

(Runs off)

RAINBOW, WHERE ARE MY SYRINGES???

Run out and face the audience.

Hey man, man, excuse me, man, I just want to tell you, man, uh, I just saw the show and it was . . . it was really intense. And I wondered if I could ask you a question? I've been taking this course on performance from Willem Dafoe, well actually from this woman who used to work with Willem Dafoe and uh, she's been teaching us about breathing and honesty in breathing and I was watching you tonight, man, and uh, you breathe so honestly, man.

And I was wondering uh, could I buy you a cup of coffee, man, we could just hang out and rap for an hour or two?

Oh, yeah of course, cool, cool. I understand. No, you're busy, that's cool.

I just want to tell you, man, that I think your shit's great. And uh, I think like you and Gary Oldman and Steven Seagal are doing like the only interesting shit out there right now. I mean it, I think you're a genius.

Me? I make performances like you. I mean, not like *you*. But uh, like you. It's funny, like some of the shit you do out there, man, it's like you've been to one of my shows and you're like stealing my shit. I mean I know you're not . . .

But I wish you could come see what I do, man. I like perform and I have this friend who does this music while I'm performing because you know you have to have music with your shit for like marketing purposes and stuff, you know? They won't put you on MTV if you don't have music. I mean, you don't have to worry about that shit, you're old and every-thing . . .

But I wish you could see it. I know you'd dig it.

I do this one thing, where I take this human skull and I cover it all with cheese food until it looks like a real head and I stick it on this stick and stick the stick on like this spring on my back and like when I'm jumping around the head is like bouncing around and I'm like: "Whoa! A *head*!" And I grab it and I bite it and all the skin's like falling off and the audience gets totally grossed out . . . and . . .

Oh! And last week, man, you would have loved this. . . . We went down to the meat market and we got all these pigs' guts and blood and shit and we filled up these ziploc bags with 'em, stuck 'em under our clothes. The audience didn't even know they were there.

And we're like jumping around and doing our show and like all of a sudden we pull out these straight razors and sliced our stomachs right open and all the guts and blood are like falling out and chicks are screaming and I'm slipping on the blood. Fell down, took three stitches over my eye, man. See?

Like art imitating life.

Yeah. Yeah. That's what everybody says. My shit's intense.

But it's kind of frustrating too 'cause we play all the time in these like small places and we try to get like agents and managers and critics to come see it and they don't, it's pretty frustrating, you know?

It must be great to play a huge place like this, huh? You must have had to really hustle somebody to get in here, huh?

Like did you have an agent who set this up?

Yeah? Who's your agent? . . . William Morris, cool.

That's what I want to do, man, I want to be with William Morris and do what you did: *Use* the system to *destroy* the system. Like you, like Johnny Depp.

It's funny you should mention your agent, man, because I happen to have this video with me of my stuff. . . .

Well, wait a minute, man, I'm talking to you, man. Don't walk away from me like that. It's like I'm some kind of jerk or something. I'm just trying to honestly tell you how I feel, I mean isn't that what your work's about or are you some kind of hypocrite or something?

Yeah, I understand you have someplace to go, man, I have someplace to go too, but I'm taking the time out to talk to you. The least you could do . . .

Oh, wait a minute, what's that look, man? What's that look? OH! I forgot, you're more important than me! Oh, I'm sorry!!! You're a big deal and I'm not.

(Angry)

Hey man, lemme tell you something, just because you get your name in the paper and you get to play all these big places, doesn't mean that you're like better than me, man. OK? My shit is just as important as your shit, OK? I don't need to get my name in the paper for my shit to be important.

That's what I'm saying. That's what I'm saying. Right. So basically our shit is equal. So why don't you give your agent the tape? I mean didn't anybody ever give you a helping hand when you were starting out?

(Pause. Mime receiving something)

Oh, no, oh, that would be cool. So this is like your agent? This is his name? Thanks, man. So I just drop off the tape and he'll like look at it and maybe like have a meeting with me and shit. Great.

Hey, hey, listen man, thank you so much and uh, listen, it would mean so much to me if you would come by one night and see my show. You know what, we're playing this week. I'll put your name on the guest list . . . plus one, come on by, you know, bring your agent if you want to. It's going to be a really great gig. I ran into Harvey Keitel on the street the other day and uh, you know, he might be coming. And I sent a letter to Christian Slater. He hasn't written me back, but he'll probably be there too. You never know, you might meet those guys there, be a good career move for you.

Oh, OK. I gotta get going now too, I'm busy, too.

But listen, I'll give my number to your agent and you know if you ever need to talk to me about anything, you need advice or anything, just gimme a call. I have voice mail.

(Backing away)

OK, man, OK. OK. Good luck, man. See you at the gig.

Man walks toward the edge of the stage, pointing with a long stainless-steel cooking fork.

So what we did, we put a chain-link fence around the whole fifteen acres. Barbed wire on top. For security, for security. 'Cause you know, Charlie, we're here all summer, the kids are running around in the yard. I sleep better at night just knowing it's out there.

Oh, yeah, we're here all summer. I go down the city maybe two, three times a month. But you know it's hot down there and we got everything we need up here. The pool. Sonia's got her tennis court, I got my griller. I just stay here all summer and grill. I put everything on this thing: steaks, chops, chicken. Last Sunday, I did some lobsters. Came out beautiful. Once they stop moving, they're a snap to cook.

Did you look at my grill, Charlie? Look at my grill. Brand new, I just got it. It's beautiful. See, right here where the steaks are, this is the grilling part. Then over here I got two stovetops, you wanna boil some peas, carrots. Underneath, oven. You can bake a cake, cookies, whatever you want.

Up here, microwave oven. Ice chest on the side, 'frigerator on the back. Three phone lines.

Very reasonable, around three grand. Got it from the Hammacher-Schlemmer catalog. I love it. I just stand here all summer and grill. Very relaxing, I just stay here by the pool, they swim, I grill. Makes me very mellow. Like meditating.

(Shouts off)

WHAT?!! Nah, we don't want any. . . . You want any goat cheese? Charlie doesn't want any either. I don't care what you did to it, we *hate* goat cheese. Listen, honey, we're starving to death out here, send out some Doritos or something. Well, if you're too busy, Jeremy can bring 'em.

(Calling to a different part of the stage)

Jeremy, honey, go up to Mommy on the porch, get Daddy and Uncle Charlie some Doritos.

(Back to "Sonia")

He can do it, Sonia, just give him the Doritos. Give him the Doritos! Don't give him the goat cheese!

(To "Charlie")

Why would anybody eat goat cheese? We went to a farm one time. You see what goats eat? Who knows what's in that stuff?

Oh yeah, he loves it. He's in there all day. Like a fish. No.

No. No. No. There's no chlorine in that pool, Charlie. They use chlorine in the *cheap* pools. This filter, this is the *best* you can get. Fourteen layers of charcoal, three layers of sand. Then there's a machine, you can't see it, under the tennis courts, boils the water into steam, sterilizes it drop by drop.

Comes back to the pool, completely pure. Completely pure. You can't get water like that in *nature.*

'Cause I figure we got people coming over every weekend. Somebody's gonna come over, do a couple of laps. Guy's got herpes, next thing I know everybody in the house has herpes. What do you do with a six-year-old with herpes? I figure spend the money, get the filter. Why waste the aggravation?

'Cause you know, Charlie, I'm at that time in my life, I don't want to spend the money on the crazy stuff anymore. Remember, I used to have that car, that Porsche? What did it cost me? Hundred grand, plus a grand a month for insurance, parking? I never drove the damn thing. Sat in the garage. No, well, I don't drive a stick.

Now, I spend the money on the good things in my life: my family, the house. Spend it on the garden, the pool, the kids. You know that's what's important. I want to enjoy the kids while they're still young.

Of course, I got the other kids from the other marriages. Uh . . . Bobby just turned twenty-five. Finally graduated college. And Nancy, she's a sophomore. She's shacked up someplace with her boyfriend for the summer. And little Frank, baby Frank, from the other marriage, he's fourteen now. Can you believe it?

But you know, those kids, I want to say to those kids: "GO AWAY!" You know? Your *mother* hates me, *you* hate me, so leave me alone. Here's a check, get lost!

I mean, Sonia and I have a good thing now, since the therapy. Little Jeremy, you saw him, he's a good kid. And little, uh, Genevieve, you see her running around in her bathing suit, so cute.

I got a good life. I never want to leave the house. I had to go to the city last week, visit a client, it was *torture*. It was like going off to war.

I mean you go down there now, it's like the black hole of Calcutta. You been down there lately? It's depressing. They're lying on the streets, begging, on drugs. With the babies, now they're begging. I feel so bad for those poor people, 'cause it's not their fault.

But what can you say? Life isn't fair. It's the roll of the dice, they're *fucked*. I didn't make up the rules. I just say thank God he loves us.

(Fiddles with the "cooking steaks")

I'm stopped at a stoplight, down Houston Street, and this character is washing my windshield and I'm looking up at him through the glass. I can see his face and I start fantasizing. We had this stuff in Vietnam, napalm. You know what napalm is? Jellied gasoline. I have this fantasy, I'm in a helicopter, just flying down the Bowery, I spray 'em, drop a match, put 'em all outta their misery. They wouldn't even know what hit 'em. I'm not saying it's a solution. I mean it's a solution, it's not *the* solution. You wouldn't actually do it.

You like roast peppers?

(Stabs downward, then holds the fork up)

Look at this pepper, isn't it beautiful? Balducci's, five bucks each, the best you can get. I'll have one too.

See, I keep 'em on ice over here in the ice chest, anytime I want peppers, I . . . WHAT?

YES! PUT THE CORN ON *NOW*. PUT THE CORN ON NOW, SONIA! THE STEAK'S GONNA BE READY IN FIVE MINUTES. YOU WANT COLD STEAK? I'M ASKING, YOU WANT COLD STEAK? THEN PUT THE CORN ON NOW!

Did I tell you about last spring when we went on vacation? No, I know you know we went on vacation, but let me tell you . . .

About three weeks before we go away, I'm working in midtown around Forty-eighth Street. And every day, I go out to lunch, stretch my legs. And every day there's this guy in front of the building with one of those signs: "WILL WORK FOR FOOD." Begging. So every day, I pass this guy, I give him a quarter, I figure, I can afford it.

The guy gets used to seeing me. Every day at lunch, sees me coming, kinda gets all perky when he sees me. Gets up on his hind legs.

So about a week before we're gonna go on vacation, I go out to lunch, I see the guy, guy sees me, I reach into my pocket, I don't have any change! He's looking at me. So I figure, what the hell, who's it gonna kill? Give the guy a buck.

I throw a buck at the guy. Turns out, it's not a buck, it's a twenty-dollar bill. Don't ask me how it happened. Guy jumps up, starts shaking my hand, blessing me, telling me God loves me, Jesus loves me. Shaking my hand in the middle of the sidewalk. And I never really looked at this guy up close before. He's got all these sores all over his face, no teeth, his breath could peel paint. And I'm thinking, you know: "I gave you the money, now go back and sit down!"

Anyway, I forget about the guy; three days later, me and

Sonia go down to St. Barth's. . . . Very nice hotel by the beach, they give you a brochure about the food and how there's these dolphins and you lie on the beach and watch the dolphins. Seven hundred dollars a night.

We get down there, I'm a little tense, I want to relax, so we go down the beach. I'm lying there, looking for the dolphins, no dolphins. I'm getting a strain in my neck. Turns out, there's no dolphins in the Caribbean. I'm in litigation with the hotel as I speak.

Anyway, we're lying there, Sonia says, "What's that?" She's pointing to my hand. There's this rash on the back of my hand. I say, I don't know, poison ivy from the country house. Forget about it.

Charlie, by the end of the week, this rash is halfway up my arm. We come back to the city, I go straight to my doctor's.

He says, "Good thing you came to see me. If you hadn't come to see me, that would have gone right up your arm, up your neck, into your eyes. You'd be *blind!*" Turns out . . . RIGHT! THAT'S RIGHT! The *guy.* Turns out, it's some kind of disease they give each other in the men's shelter. Some kind of bum disease.

All I'm saying, Charlie, all I'm saying is: I give the guy money, he gives me a disease!

(Looks up)

Jeremy, what are doing? No, honey, don't throw Doritos in the pool. Get away from the pool, YOU'RE GONNA CLOG UP THE FILTER IT'S GONNA COST ME FIFTY THOUSAND DOLLARS, NOW GET AWAY FROM THE POOL. JUST GO SOMEWHERE.

(Back to "Charlie")

I ever tell you about my friend, George, down on Wall Street?
Now, here's a guy, about three years ago, makes a killing.
Shorts some stock, makes fifteen million dollars on one deal.
Says to himself: "That's it, I win." Gets off the street. Goes
down to the South Pacific, buys an island. They're not that
expensive, about two million bucks. Moves his whole family
down the island.

I'm talking to him on the phone yesterday, says it's great
down there. Beautiful weather every day. Inexpensive. He's
got a satellite dish, gets a hundred and fifty stations. Gets it
all: *Seinfeld*, the Knicks. No problems with parking, car
hijacking, drugs . . . it's his own island, he's the king of the
island. And I know how he feels . . .

I mean, look, I'm the world's biggest liberal. But you know
I'm watching that CNN, I'm watching those riots in L.A. and
I'm thinking to myself: "What if they start doing that around
here? What if they start running around like that around
here?"

I mean, look at this house, Charlie. You can't see this house
from the road. We're vulnerable up here. What happens,
we're up here one Sunday, we're hanging out: reading the
paper, eating bagels, grinding coffee beans. I pick up the
phone to call my mother: "Oh, the phone is dead!"

I look up, a couple of black guys are at the back door.
Breaking down the back door. They don't even have to be
black guys, could be anybody. Then what do I do? What do
I do then? "Oh, come on in, would you like a cup of coffee?
Maybe you'd like to rape my wife, kill my kids, burn my
house down?"

What do I do then, Charlie? What do I do then?

That's why I have the gun.

(Fiddles with "steak")

I would, I would shoot them, for the kids I would shoot. If they were from the phone company, I would still shoot them.
    Anyways, these are ready.

(Calls off)

Jeremy, honey, come out of the bushes, Daddy's not angry anymore. Come on out, we'll discuss it later. We're gonna have din-din now. No, no hot dogs, we've got fifteen-dollar-a-pound prime sirloin from Dean & DeLuca, now come out of the bush. COME ON! COME IN THE HOUSE!

Raise hand.

Me? Oh . . .

(Sit down on floor, cross-legged)

Hello, my name is Eric and I'm a recovering male.

And I just want to share that I agree with what Tim was just saying about feeling shame for his penis. I think alot of my masculinity issues are very shame-based. In fact it's funny, when Tim was sharing just now, I was thinking of all the times I've been in the shower in the morning and I'll look down at my penis and it will remind me of what a bad person I've been.

But I'm glad Tim brought this up, because this is something I've been trying to get in touch with.

(Laughs to himself)

Not my penis, of course. Although that has been an issue for me in the past. Well, when I was very small, my, uh, mother would whip me with a phone cord whenever I, uh, touched myself down there and uh, it's only been recently that I've stopped getting erections whenever the phone rang.

But I want to talk about where I'm at today. I'm in a good place today. I just completed a course at the New School, "Your Self, Your Shame, Your Orgasm." Yes, it was very good, you should try it. Because you know, I used to just worry about my own orgasm, and now I worry about everyone's orgasm.

But I feel so stuck sometimes.

Like on my way here tonight. This beautiful girl walks by me on the street and she's got this really tight sweater on, you know. Kind of large breasts. Jiggling. And I can't help myself, I have to check out her breasts.

(Mimes the move)

Like some kind of Pavlovian dog! And then once she's walked past me I have to check out her butt! Like I've never seen a butt before!

It's depressing. I feel like a human being trapped in a man's body!

So anyway, about two weeks ago, this friend of mine gets these tickets to go see this woman he knows do this concert at Carnegie Hall. So he asks me to go along. This woman is a pianist . . . *pi*anist. And I don't really know anything about classical music, but I go and it's great. She's playing all this stuff–Bach, Chopin–and I'm blown away.

So afterwards there's this reception for her at this apartment, so I tag along with my friend. And I'm just hanging out, next thing I know, he's bringing her over to introduce her to me. So I'm shaking her hand and she's got these beautiful brown eyes and beautiful smile and she's got this evening gown on and she smells great and she's just done this fabulous concert and I'm shaking her hand and all I can think about is: "I would love to have sex with this woman." SO INAPPROPRIATE! I mean, where does that shit come from?

I was so ashamed. I was ashamed of my shame. I ran out of the room, locked myself in the bathroom in this apartment. People are pounding on the door. I'm crying . . . I'm trying to cry. Fortunately I had my portable John Bradshaw with me.

Anyway I was sharing this with my therapist last week and she suggested that I write a letter to one of the women I fantasize about when I uh, masturbate. Not send it, just write it. So I did and she said it was good and then she said I should read it to my group.

So here's this letter:

(Pulls letter out of pocket and reads it)

Dear Michelle,

First of all I don't know if your name is Michelle or not, but that is what I call you. Maybe we will meet someday and I will be able to learn your real name.

Maybe I will see you walking down the street, or in a subway, or maybe I will sit down in a movie theater and you will be sitting next to me. I hope it will happen, because then I will be able to apologize to you for all the harm I've done.

You are probably thinking: How could you have done me any harm, I don't even know you. And I know that

that's true. Probably hundreds of thousands of men fantasize about you every week. So in that way, I know I'm not special.

But I have to apologize.

Every Sunday I tear through the magazine supplements looking for you. Where is she? Where is Michelle? I look for you in the lingerie ads, the health club ads, the Club Med ads. I get frantic and then finally, every week I find you. Yes! In a string bikini, in a matching bra and girdle combo, maybe reclining in a steamy bathtub full of bubbles, almost revealing a nipple!

And then you are mine, all mine.

I hate to tell you what I do, but you belong to me, and I have you in every way I can think of . . . I consume you. I turn you inside out. You are my willing love slave and I am your love master.

I relish your bum. I adore your boobs. I idolize your succulent . . . uh . . . vagina! I am in heaven.

Sometimes it lasts a long time, sometimes it's only a few seconds, but I have you and let me tell you, you are *wonderful.*

And then, as always, I *debase* you. At the very moment of sheer joy, I can't hold back and my lifeforce splashes onto the very thing I love, your image, your picture. You are lost once more, covered in the product of my sticky love.

I'm sorry, I really am. But I love you just the same. I'm just a man with a penis. And for that I'm sorry.

(Stands up and puts the letter away)

And that's it, thanks for letting me share. I don't want anyone to share back to me, thank you.

Stands, calls off.

David come on in, sit down. Sit down.

(Gets a chair for himself, picks up prescription pad)

We got the results back from the lab and they're good, they're good, lots of positive indicators. I'll let you take them home with you when you leave, you can look at them in your free time.

(Sits)

Sit down, David, sit down. Now David, just to be on the safe side, I'd like to start you on some medication. I can't say it's going to do anything but on the other hand, it can't hurt either.

(Scribbles on pad)

Now, this is a very common prescription item. I've prescribed it many times before. Just take this down to the pharmacy and you should have no trouble getting it filled.

Now, there are *some* side effects. Just want you to know what they are, in case anything comes up, you don't get overly concerned. OK?

(Scribbles)

Now, David, let me ask you this, do you drink milk? . . . Well, in your coffee in the morning, or on your cereal, any baked goods with milk in them? Stay away from milk, OK? No milk and no eggs.

Well, because there are amino acids present in milk and eggs that can react negatively with certain proteins in the medication and on occasion cause *convulsions, seizures.* And we don't want that do we? We want you feeling better, not worse.

I'll write that down: "No milk and no eggs."

Now after you're on the medication for two or three days, you will notice some blurring of vision. Just means the medicine is working. You'll also notice a diminishment of your sex drive. . . .Well, to a great extent, to a great extent. I'd be surprised if you have any sex drive at all after a couple of weeks on this stuff.

Also, when you get up in the morning you may experience some dizziness. Don't worry about that. What you might find worrisome is that when you're taking a shower you're going to be losing some *hair.* Clumps of hair. You might get some bald spots. If this is a problem for you I would prescribe . . . I would prescribe a hat.

Itching is very common. You'll get some itching on your arms and on your legs, palms of the hands, soles of the feet. You might even get what we call an "epidermal sebaceous trauma" which is just a fancy term for large bleeding scabs on your arms and on your legs. If this is a problem, just call Heidi at the front desk and she'll give you a prescription for some hydrocortisone cream, clear that right up. I won't charge you for the visit.

Also numbness in your fingers, your toes, your ears, your nose, all your extremities.

And, how shall I say this? You may experience some temporary *blindness*. It's only temporary. You'll get up in the morning, you won't be able to see for awhile. Has no medical significance, lasts about fifteen, twenty minutes. If you wake up and you can't see, just sit on the edge of the bed, wait it out, thirty, forty-five minutes. If it doesn't clear up by that time, be sure to call me.

Also in the morning it's common to experience nausea, vomiting, incontinence. If you have trouble holding your bowels, just give Heidi a call and she'll give you something that will clear that right up.

And I tell all my patients taking this drug make sure to keep your meals *small* because you will be throwing up quite a bit.

Bleeding from the nose can be unexpected.

(Leaning back)

Actually there's a funny story. I have a patient who's been on this drug for, oh, must be four years now, and they were throwing this birthday party for him at this ritzy restaurant. You know these places, they take forever to bring the food.

He's waiting, waiting. Finally, they bring the food. He looks down at his entree, *drops of blood* start falling from his nose!!!

(Laughing, then stopping himself)

They brought him another entree, of course.

Just have a handkerchief with you at all times and if your nose starts to bleed just dab lightly, do not blow, just dab and it should clear up in . . . about fifteen minutes.

(Signs the prescription)

And that's it. We'll do some more tests in about three months, see what kind of results we're getting, if we don't like the results, we'll put you on something stronger. OK?

(Stands)

Oh, don't thank me, David, it's just the miracle of modern medicine.

Thank you, yes, got a little tan. Just got back from St. Barth's. You look good, too, David, you look very good.

(Snaps his fingers)

Oh David, I almost forgot! Well, the insurance company sent the claim back. Yes, they're not going to pay. No. So could you stop by Heidi on your way out and drop off a check today? Uh-huh, for the whole amount, the whole five thousand would be good.

OK, David, alright. OK. You too. Take care.

With quiet intensity.

Excuse me, you look confused. Did you know that there's a path out of your confusion? There is. It's your ego that causes your confusion. You are not the center of the universe. You are not God. You have to realize that you are nothing. Just as I have accepted that I am nothing.

I finally realized that I am nothing more than an ant crawling on a leaf on a vine in the middle of the Amazon jungle. I am just shit on God's shoe. But even though I am nothing, I am part of a bigger plan. And so are you.

See, like you, I used to get confused. I'd watch TV and I'd see all those rich famous people and I'd think to myself: "Why do they have everything and I have nothing?" I'd get angry. But maybe those people are being rewarded for being good? If I look at them I can see they have such nice smiles, such nice teeth. They are so beautiful, so good. No wonder good things are happening for them. They deserve it.

You see, God gives you what you deserve.

I'll be walking down the street and I'll see a person lying on the ground, in pain, and I'll think to myself: "Why is that person in pain? Why is that person suffering?" But I don't know why God put that person in my path. Maybe God is trying to teach me something? Or maybe that person did something? Maybe that person is a murderer? I don't know. Maybe, probably, probably did *something*, otherwise why is God making that person suffer?

You know there's alot of terrible things that happen to people in the world. Alot of things we can't understand. But that's the way it has to be. If everybody just did what they wanted all the time and had it easy all the time and nothing bad ever happened, we'd just be like a bunch of children having fun, and that wouldn't be any good, would it?

So don't be confused. And don't worry. Because you are part of a bigger plan. You can't understand it and you can't change it.

Have a nice day.

BLOW ME

Pacing the stage. Into a microphone, loud.

I woke up this morning and I had a big fucking headache, man! You know why I had a big fucking headache, because I got fucked-up last night, that's why!

So you know what I did when I got up this morning, man? I got fucked-up again, man! You wanna know why? 'Cause I hate the *taste* of fresh-squeezed orange juice, *man*, I hate the *smell* of fresh-ground coffee, I hate the *sound* of Bryant Gumball's voice! I hate driving to work, I hate standing up, I hate breathing, I hate waiting to die!

Why should I work a job, man? So some ASSHOLE who has nothing better to do can get off by telling *me* what to do, so that maybe, JUST MAYBE, I can take home a check for a hundred and forty-eight dollars and twenty-seven cents after they take fucking taxes out so that a bunch of lying, cheating, POLA-FUCKIN'-TICIANS can get their free *limos* and their free *haircuts* and their free *postage stamps* and their free *blow jobs*????

BLOW . . . ME.

Blow me. Blow me Bill Clinton. Blow me Hillary Rodham Clinton. Blow me Al Gore. Blow me Tipper Gore.

Why should I work a job? So maybe I can get some *fringe benefits*? So maybe I can get some *health insurance*, so that if anything really goes wrong with me, I can call up the insurance company and they'll say: "I'm sorry sir, your coverage doesn't cover stomach cancer, I'm sorry sir, your coverage doesn't cover massive brain tumors, I'm sorry sir, your coverage doesn't cover secret incurable CIA-sponsored diseases." Blow me. Blow . . . me.

I have the same dream every night when I'm not blacked out. It's World War Three and the bombs are falling onto New York and L.A. and there's this huge ultra-megaton bomb, slowly falling onto Washington, D.C.

And all the politicians, the congressmen and the Supreme court judges and the President and the Vice President are all scurrying down these secret passageways to these secret bunkers underground that they think are bombproof. But what they don't realize is that me and my friends have already stuck a whole bunch of other nuclear bombs down there in those bunkers and when they're stuck inside, we padlock all the doors and me and Lee Marvin and Charles Bronson and Trini Lopez and the rest of the Dirty Dozen go running down throwing these hand grenades down their airtubes and blow their fat asses away on golfcarts to hell.

Yeah, yeah, yeah, yeah, yeah, I have a death fantasy. This is my death fantasy: I'm driving down the highway doing about ninety miles an hour, and I have a head-on collision with a bus filled with those singing nuns from that movie *Sister Act.*

But just before I hit, I want to be shooting up heroin between my toes, and jerking off to a copy of *Hustler* magazine and listening to Howard Stern on the radio. So when I'm in the fireball burning up I'll be laughing and coming at the same time. At least I won't be bored, at least I won't be bored with all the *stimulation.*

"Oh I wonder what's on TV tonight? Maybe SOMETHING GOOD is on!"

"Did you see the latest issue of *VANITY FAIR*? Did you see what it said about WOODY FUCKING ALLEN? Did you see what it said about DEMI FUCKING MOORE? It was so FUCKING INTERESTING!"

"Don't my triceps look great, I've been working out."

"I just waxed my car! I just waxed my skis. I just waxed my legs. I just waxed my brain."

"I LOVE MOVIES WITH EMMA THOMPSON. THEY'RE SO . . . MOVING."

"OH, I'M GOING TO GET AN EARRING AND PUT IT IN MY NOSE!"

"OH, I'M GONNA GET A BASEBALL HAT AND TURN IT AROUND BACKWARDS."

"OH, I'M GONNA GET A TATTOO!"

I'm gonna get a tattoo, man, I'm gonna tattoo my *eyelids.* It's gonna say "BLOW ME" . . . so everybody knows how I feel about 'em.

OH I'M SO WORRIED ABOUT THE RECESSION!

OH I'M SO WORRIED ABOUT STARVING AFRICAN CHILDREN!

OH I'M SO WORRIED ABOUT THE PLAYOFFS!

OH I'M SO WORRIED ABOUT LYME DISEASE!

OH I'M SO WORRIED ABOUT THAT STAIN ON THE RUG!

OH, THANK GOD I'M NOT POOR!
OH, THANK GOD I'M NOT BLIND!
OH, THANK GOD I DON'T HAVE AIDS!
THANK GOD I'M NOT A FAGGOT!
THANK GOD I'M NOT A NIGGER!
Blow me. Blow me. Blow me.

I'm gonna find the biggest ugliest pig, all covered with mud, and I'm gonna take that pig and lift up its curly tail and I'm gonna grease up its asshole with vaseline. And then I'm going to get a huge hard-on and shove it in. And while that pig is squealing with joy, I'm gonna be smoking crack in a giant crack pipe while Sally Field stands behind me in a leather bondage outfit with a strap-on dildo, fucks me up the ass while she bangs me over the head with a giant wooden mallet.

It will be alot more interesting than driving my Honda Accord in the 55 mile-per-hour zone. Alot more interesting than grinding my amaretto-flavored coffee beans. Alot more interesting than setting my alarm clock to 6:15 AM. Alot more interesting than reading *Time* magazine's analysis of Ronald Reagan's colon polyps. Alot more interesting than listening to Michael Bolton sing songs of LOVE.

Hey, you know what I'm descended from, man? Animals, man. Animals are put on earth to do four things: eat, sleep, fuck and bite each other. That's it. That is what I'm genetically designed to do. Eat, sleep, fuck and bite. All the rest is extra. All the rest is some shit some little dogs made up to get in my way. Hey, if you can't run with the big dogs, stay under the porch.

I was going down the highway the other day, minding my own business and a state trooper pulls me over. He comes up to the car and he said, "Son, do you realize how fast you were driving?" I said, "Why don't you tell me—while you BLOW ME!"

I went down to the unemployment office and there's this lady sitting behind the counter, she's *eating* from this giant bag of potato chips, she's got a can of chip dip on her desk, she's dipping the chips in the chip dip. She's eating while she's talking to me. She goes, "You're not fit for employment." I said, "YOU'RE NOT FIT TO BLOW ME."

I'm standing in line for two hours to see this movie they should pay *me* to see, and this security guard in a uniform with a nightstick comes by and goes, "Get in line" "Get in line" "Get in line." I said, "GET IN LINE TO BLOW ME."

This guy comes up to me and says: "Have you heard the good news, God loves you." I said, "Look, I met God, and he's a five-foot-tall Chinese transvestite with AIDS and he told me to tell you to BLOW ME!"

I'm going through a change of lifestyle, I'm going to change my lifestyle.

I'm going to stop bathing, stop brushing my teeth, stop wiping my ass. I'm going to smell so bad people are going to smell me before they *see* me. They're gonna run away when they smell me coming.

I'm going to overeat. I'm going to eat ten Sara Lee cakes every day, all covered with whipped cream and melted butter. Four or five a day. I'm gonna get so fat that when fat people see me, I'm gonna *cheer them up.*

I'm going to be a junkie, take every drug: crack, Prozac, Advil, Children's Tylenol. I'm gonna be so bad, strung-out junkies are gonna see me and go: "There but for the grace of God go I."

I'm going to hang out in shopping malls and become a serial killer. Have a freezer in my basement full of body parts.

I'm gonna bring them up piece by piece, put 'em in the microwave, cook 'em and eat 'em while I watch tapes of the last episode of *CHEERS*!

(Falls to his knees)

I want you to shave my hair off, peel my skin off, wrap me up in rusty razor wire and whip my feet so that maybe I can feel something real for just two or three seconds. So that maybe, just maybe I can CLEAR MY HEAD OF ALL THE NOISE!

(Pounds head on floor)

ORPHANS

In order to make a piece like Pounding Nails, *I have to dish up a number of improvs and monologues, then edit them down to the particular dozen that make up the show. A few of those that get cut, I like so much I want to share them. These are the orphans.*

LITTLE DOG

All I need is what I want! Park me in front of a TV set, give me something semi-meaningful to do, tell me I'm a good dog and I'll wag my tail. I'm not asking for too much. Give me some table scraps, a fresh bowl of water, throw me a bone, I'll be your friend forever.

I just don't want to be left behind. I see green lawns, I want green lawns! I know a dog who has a tennis racket, I want one too! I read about one dog who makes over a million dollars a year. Me too, me too! Don't leave me behind. I just want to be able to run around, hold my head high and piss on things. That's all. Give me a Mercedes Benz, it doesn't have to be the *biggest* one. Send me stacks of catalogs in the mail. Give me a toll-free number and a gold American Express card. I just want to be one of the pack.

I know a dog, a very good friend of mine, his owner takes him for walks, lets him shit on the ground and then the owner bends over and picks up his shit!!! I'm telling you the truth! I saw it with my own eyes! And I'm not asking for that! I have higher aspirations!

Give me art! I like art. Art is cool. Art gives meaning to my life. Through art I communicate with my fellow dogs. Through art I transcend my petty existence and am able to face another day of Alpo. Plus art makes me rich and famous. Which I like alot.

When I'm rich and famous I feel like a big and strong doggie. I get to bark at all the other dogs and be a bastard and hump all the bitches. Which I like alot.

But I don't really want to be the BIGGEST dog. Then all the other dogs will try to assassinate me. And I don't want to be the smallest dog either, because then all the other dogs piss on me.

I just want to be a middle dog. I want to be one of the pack, a face in the crowd, a member of the gang, an ingredient, a component, a cog in the wheel. That's what I am, a cog!

I am a cog dog.

(Barks)

Cog dog, cog dog, cog dog cog.

I just want to be able to run with the other guys and chase cars. Is that asking too much? No. I say, "No."

Look, it's a dog-eat-dog world out there. Life's unfair. Life's a bitch and then they put you to sleep. I didn't make the rules, I just try to live by them.

I was lying on the couch, watching TV the other day, engaged in some creative channel-surfing when this guy came on. He was on all the stations at the same time. He said:

"My Fellow Americans, the only thing we have to fear is fear itself. Sure the country's in tough shape. Sure things are scary. But everything will turn out all right. It's not a question of *when* are things going to get better, or *how* are things going to get better but *who*. Who will save us. And so we must ask ourselves: 'Who are we as a people?'" And so I must ask myself: "Who am I" and the answer, I think, is obvious: "Rowf! Rowf! Rowf!"

OK Stacey, now make love to the camera, make love to the
camera . . . now spread, spread, that's good, get into it, get
into it, more tongue, arch your back, good, look at the camera, close your eyes, you're in ecstasy, more, more, more,
more, more, more, more! That's it. Now spread the cheeks,
spead the cheeks, stay in the light! Good! Excellent! Wait a
minute, CUT! Where's makeup? Re-do her lips, they're all
wrong! No! Not those you idiot! Yes, right, more pouting,
more innocent. Thank you. And re-rouge the nipples, they're
all smeared. Good, OK, is she wet enough? Where's Tony?
TONY! Come on! More vaseline, please! Do I have to do
everything myself? Come on, hurry up, she's drier than the
Grand Canyon! We need moisture here, I'm getting thirsty
just looking at her! OK, good, Stacey? Alright, alright, where
was I? I'm getting confused here . . . so now, Stacey, you're
languid, you're erotic, you're languidly erotic . . . now you're
turning over on your stomach, right, good, hugging your pil-

low and now just sort of push your little buns up in the air, there . . .

Your motivation? Your motivation is the hundreds of thousands of American men and women sitting in their homes who need you to take them by the hand and reveal to them the secrets of erotic salvation! Look into the camera lens, because they're out there with their TV sets and VCRs. Can you see them? They need you, Stacey, to lead them to ecstasy, so don't let them down. OK? Good!

Now, where's the guy? Bring in the guy. Where is he? Yeah, you, Hoss, come here, what's your name? Chuck? Chuck you know what they call that in France? A "baguette." Just joking . . . could you make it a little harder please? OK, good, stop, that's enough. Jesus. Where'd they find you anyway? The Port Authority men's room? OK, now, bring it into the frame, bring it in. Is it in? Stacey are you ready? OK ACTION!

OK Chuck, go to work . . .

Come on Stacey, let's . . . yes . . . you want it, you want it, let's see the look on the face, the gratitude, the tears are running down the cheeks. . . . You're in ecstasy, you've never had anybody as erotically incredible as, uh, Chuck here before in your life. . . . GREAT! That's it, now you've got it, wonderful! Wonderful!

Come on Chuck, let's pump it! Make it count! Come on buddy, giddy up there boy! You need anything? Some hay, a sugar cube? Come on! That's it, put the leg up over the. . . . There we go, there we go! That's it, now we've got it! Are you getting all this? Get it, Johnny, come on, they're not going to do it all day! Come on, there we go. Don't run out of steam there Chuck-o! This shot is gorgeous! Beautiful. Oh, this is wonderful. This is art! This is acting! A classic! Stacey, I've never seen you better. Great acting, great performing. Who needs Meryl Streep when I've got you, Stacey! Lovely, oh, I'm coming, myself, I'm coming myself! Oh, oh, OH! Fantastic, great! Cut, relax you two, great work. Tony, hose 'em down. Did you get all that? How was it for you? You think so? OK . . . yeah. . . . Alright Stacey? Chuck? That was a great take, really terrific. . . . We're gonna try it once more like this, doggie-style, then we move on to the close-ups and the money shot. OK? Excellent!

THE DREAM

So I have to tell you about this dream I had last night. I'm fucking my grandmother right? It's just a dream. OK? So, I'm fucking my grandmother and I'm like doing her solid, she's screaming, her toes are in my ears. One of those kind of dreams, OK? And all of a sudden I look up and there is Clarence Thomas, in all his Supreme Court justice robes and things, looking down at me drinking a can of Coke. Right? Except he's got this enormous hard-on thrusting out between the folds of his robes, right into his face. And he's saying, "You can't do that!" And I'm thinking: "Aren't you supposed to be like in Washington, D.C. helping to kick-start the Fourth Reich or something? I mean, I'll do what I want, it's my privacy." But I can't say any of this, because you know how in a dream, sometimes you can't talk? Well, I couldn't talk, but the reason I couldn't talk was because his dick was in my mouth, so I'm like . . . wah-wah-wah-wah-wah. . . . Right? And I look down, and I'm not doing my grandmother anymore, now it's Madonna. In like this rubber thing with

buckles and snaps and little holes all over the place. And you
know, I'm thinking: "Cool." I'll take Madonna over my grandmother any day. But now the door bursts open and it's Jesse
Helms. But he's wearing like a Victoria's Secret lavender
nightgown with like the nipples cut out and nipple rings and
shit and plus he's wearing these knee-high Nazi jackboots.
Right? And I'm thinking, this man has never had any taste
whatsoever, I mean, a lavender nightgown with jackboots.
And he's got a camcorder and he's jumping up and down
shouting, "I got you now! I got you now, you secular human-
ist!" And just at that moment, the door bursts open again and
this time it's George Washington and Abraham Lincoln, who
were both pretty tall guys, but now they look alot taller
because they're both naked and they have these incredible
steroided muscle bodies, all oiled up, and each guy has a
massive erection, and they just come over and start butt-
fucking Jesse and Clarence with like no grease or lotion,
nothing, not even spit. They were wearing condoms though.
And then, I don't know, more and more people kept coming in: Leona Helmsley and Kurt Waldheim, and Ricky
Schroeder, and Ricky Nelson and Kim Bassinger and Hayley
Mills and Artie, this dog who got run over by the school bus
when I was ten and I don't know, a million people. Sally Field
and Oliver Stone. Malcolm X. And just more and more people kept coming in, until like the whole room was shaking
with the hot sex we were having and then everyone had this
gigantic simultaneous orgasm and I woke up.

And I was in my bed in this cold sweat and I thought, "Oh
no, I'm a homo." And I went into a panic! I said, "I'm not prej-
udiced or anything but I don't want to be a homosexual!
I . . . uh my lifestyle wouldn't support it. I'm . . . I'm too busy.
I don't have time for all the parades!"

I was in the airport the other day and I looked around me and I saw hundreds and hundreds of people running, waiting, waiting to run, running to wait. They were standing in ticket lines, they were sitting in the departure lounge, they were crowded around the luggage carousel. They were washing and flushing in the smelly restrooms. They were drinking in the bar area sitting on the bent chrome and naugahyde furniture as they watched the color TVs hanging from the ceiling. They were eating in the snack area. Being served by the sullen Mexicans and Pakistanis shoveling out tacos and nachos and hot dogs and doughnuts and pizza to middle-class white Americans who chewed furiously like rodents before they dragged their dirty little spoiled children from Cleveland to Orlando to Denver to Philly to L.A.

Waiting and waiting, always alert. Waiting to board the plane, waiting to take off, waiting for the seat-belt light to go out, waiting for the drink cart, waiting for the dinner entree, waiting for the onboard feature film, waiting for the aircraft to land and praying silently, every one of them to his or her own secret god, that the tin monster doesn't swim into some wacky air current and drag them sideways down the runway like one gigantic scraping aluminum fireball millions of other white middle-class Americans can watch on the evening news.

I want to be Oprah, I want to be Axl, I want to be Mick, I want to be Madonna. I want to be above the lines, above the crowds. Loved by millions, never touched by one. Never again to be crushed in the fray, everyone would know me, but from afar!

There's another world and I can see it. It floats above us. Call it heaven, call it Valhalla, call it Mount Olympus! Whatever you call it, the Gods are there. I can see Mount Olympus, I can see the Gods playing volleyball! Yes, there's Oliver Stone passing off to Bill Cosby! There's Steve Tyler waving to Kevin Costner. There's Oprah blowing kisses to Lady Di! I'm down here on earth, but I can see them. I can see them up there. And I want to be up there too!

Who needs drugs? Who needs money? Dentists have money! No, there's something better, there's a place made of cotton wool and sugar icing where the love of millions shines like a sun that never sets! Where everyone flies and no one walks! Where every thought, every emotion is a special event! Guilt, love and charity are precious indulgences, savored, always sweet, never sour.

Millions will understand: I'm always right and never wrong! They will say, "You know, we don't/you show, we follow! We want what you have!"

What luxury! I would fly everywhere. Just stretch my arms out and fly! And I would look down, way down at the ground and I would see the millions of tiny ants and their toy-like existence. Waiting to run and running to wait. I would float on a cloud and looking down I would think: "It doesn't look too bad from far away, I'll make a point and visit some day!" And then I would lean back and close my eyes and stretch my arm out and ring a tiny silver bell. And a small brown man would come running with a hot slice of pizza on a silver tray. And I'd take a bite and look over and wave at George Bush and I'd say: "You're right George! It does taste better up here!"